11-Step Formula to Bridge the Gap Between Parents and Teenagers

11-Step Formula to Bridge the Gap Between Parents and Teenagers

The results are incredibly rewarding!

Is the table too long or too narrow?

What do you think?

Written by Ana H.B. Weber, U.S.A.
www.anatherelationshipexpert.com

Illustrations by Storm, England
www.stormdesignprint.com

iUniverse, Inc.
New York Lincoln Shanghai

**11-Step Formula to Bridge the Gap
Between Parents and Teenagers
The results are incredibly rewarding!
Is the table too long or too narrow?
What do you think?**

iUniverse books may be ordered through booksellers or by contacting:

iUniverse
2021 Pine Lake Road, Suite 100
Lincoln, NE 68512
www.iuniverse.com
1-800-Authors (1-800-288-4677)

ISBN-13: 978-0-595-40717-0 (pbk)
ISBN-13: 978-0-595-85082-2 (ebk)
ISBN-10: 0-595-40717-X (pbk)
ISBN-10: 0-595-85082-0 (ebk)

Printed in the United States of America

I dedicate this book to all the parents and teenagers around the world.

These years are special and unique.

Make the very best of it.

I surely did, and if I could turn back the clock, I would do it all over again.

Ana H.B. Weber

CONTENTS

INTRODUCTION

I had wondered for quite some time where we can go to take a class on parenting. If we look, we can find courses and schools for almost everything desired and imagined. So, why didn't anyone come up with a lifetime course in PARENTING?

The answer is very simple. Parenting is unique. It stands out as an entity of its own. One cannot come up with a course designed and tailored for every single parent in the world. Parenting is chapters of life happening to you without advanced notice, and with every child it becomes a challenge of another kind. Indeed, parenting is original and special. As parents, we cannot plan ahead of time for things that happen, overcoming feelings and obstacles created by life. Therefore, we cannot adopt the same attitude and behavior towards everyone—children or parents. It is a complexity that will never be completely solved. The pages of our lives are flipping too quickly with so many factors impacting us, old and new feelings arising within us throughout the journey. Children grow up fast, and with every step of the way, life encircles them with power and magnitude. We also learn that we actually do change from year to year, and our children do as well.

Now can we truly keep up with that and everything else around us? Even if we had 30 hours a day instead of 24, the task would be impossible.

There is only one thing that we can repeat that will never grow old. We can express our love with our actions, our understanding, and our experiences for our kids and for ourselves.

The role of a parent can never be black and white, and a child's desires and goals cannot be measured with the same device. It is a completely different measuring system.

When the teenage years approach, the teen is completely taken by hormonal changes, the impact of the environment, home life, school life, economic status, and social circles with which they surround themselves. On top of all that, there is so much expected of them, and they seem to be so overwhelmed at times.

I ask myself:

Is this our love for them? Do we give them more than shelter, food, money for entertainment, a cell phone, etc.?

Indeed that is not nearly enough. Our time, patience, communication, attention, support, and experience are what they truly need. Can we give them all of that and keep up with our own responsibilities and happiness?

Yes, we can.

We are all aware that today's teenagers have too much to struggle with, and parents seem to grow further away from them.

There is a path we can all choose to walk on, individually and together.

We must appreciate the gift of life and the joy of the family. Live and enjoy the NOW. Examine and pull yourself into the situation you are facing (parents and teenagers) and detach your emotions and your presence from it. Watch it as though you were observing someone else's challenge and deal with it right there. Do not sweep things under the rug, hoping that they will resolve themselves. They cannot. We should not run away from our own reality, all that we built for ourselves. We are accountable and responsible for our own deeds. Don't be too hard on yourself and try not to dwell on yesterday. It is gone, far away from you.

Smile more often. Hug and kiss your kids anytime you feel like it. Talk to them and put them at ease about coming to you with questions.

Parenting is not knowledge or a subject we can find in textbooks. It is an enduring state of understanding while we grow together with our kids.

We can place small and shiny light bulbs throughout the tunnel where we walk our lives alone; with enthusiasm, exuberance, and passion they will stay bright, keeping us company as we enter, exit, and each and every step of the way.

Keep love around you. Remind yourself of that when you steer off in the opposite direction. Catch the feeling and bring it back. It will take you as high as you aim.

Thank you,

Ana H.B. Weber

FORMULA I

Parents and Teenagers: Spend one to two hours a week together—QUALITY TIME—outside your home.

Pick one:

- Restaurant

- Park

- Beach

- Mountains

- Walking

- Coffee shop

- Hiking

- Sitting by the pool

- Relaxing

On the Streets of Hollywood

Celia is a partner in a law firm. It took her ten years to achieve her dream position after she took the bar and passed it on the first try.

At the age of 37, she is one among many executive-career, single moms in Los Angeles. The hefty paycheck she receives gives her the freedom to drive a new BMW every two years, own a spacious condo close to the beach, and wear stylish clothes. Once a year she takes a short vacation to Europe or Asia. She has quite a bit to juggle: a demanding career, parenthood, and other responsibilities and amusements. But Celia considers herself a woman with many talents, and the most delicate one is the way she is handling her 16-year-old daughter, Amanda. Celia loves her with her whole heart and considers Amanda the best souvenir from her three-year marriage to Tim. He was never too gracious with anything, especially the commitment he broke six months after Amanda was born.

During the week, Celia gets home around 8:30 p.m., and she works weekends, too, when she needs to add an extra touch to a case or wrap up material for a trial.

Regardless of the long working hours, she loves her career and proves to be very good at everything she does.

Occasionally, Celia would date on weekends or she would see close friends from the firm for dinner, movie, or a visit to the local theater. She would rather not get involved with anyone in a serious way. Her independence is too valuable to her, and getting Amanda ready for college is her second priority. Perhaps in a few years she will be ready for a partner, but for now, she would rather keep it simple and uncomplicated.

Saturday mornings, Celia runs the normal errands: dry cleaners, grocery shopping, etc. Needless to say, mother-daughter quality moments were not happening too often in their household. But all that changed one Friday night.

Amanda was supposed to be sleeping at her friend Francis's house, and Celia never bothered questioning or calling there for her. She made dinner and movie plans with an old friend for that night. Mark used to work with her at the law firm where they both started their careers—two inexperienced lawyers, exuberant and excited with the opportunity and the fresh start.

Celia enjoyed seeing Mark from time to time. So much had happened in their lives since those early days.

That Friday night, they went out for Italian veal with pasta, and after devouring their food, they made their way out of the cozy restaurant and drove directly to the movie theater in Century City.

The outing came to an end, and by then it was after midnight. As soon as Celia got behind the wheel, she felt tired and sleepy. She entered her home eager to go to bed as soon as she washed her face, brushed her teeth, and peeled off the semi-casual clothes she loved to wear away from work.

At two a.m., the phone on her nightstand rang unexpectedly, abruptly waking her up, interrupting her sleep. At first, she thought it was a loud dream, but when the voice on the line sounded so deep and clear, she knew it was real.

The man on the phone identified himself as a police officer and then got right to the point, "Your daughter, Amanda, is here at the station. Would you please come down?"

That second, Celia knew that trouble had been knocking, but she never expected it to be so overwhelming and unkind. She put on the same clothes she had worn earlier that evening and, with trembling hands, picked up her keys and purse. All she wanted was to see that Amanda was safe and bring her back home where she belonged.

As she arrived at the station, she was amazed by what she saw. Amanda's face was covered with full makeup, red lipstick darker than she would ever use on herself, hair topped with a long blonde wig teased up high. She wore tight, purple boots with four-inch heels, a pink miniskirt, and a low-cut top worn off her bare shoulders.

Celia was too shocked to speak at first. She could not believe her eyes. Was this her little girl?

Standing there, a total stranger, Amanda started to cry uncontrollably. "Please forgive me, Mom," she said while her mascara ran down her cheeks, and she watched her mother's face, flushing with anger. They stared at each other—too many questions in their minds to make even the slightest sound.

The policeman spoke up. "We found your daughter standing next to a prostitute in Hollywood. They were stopping some of the cruising cars looking for business, if you know what I mean," he said with an unpleasant look on his face. He added, "We will release her to you tonight, but you better make sure that this incident will never happen again. I understand that you are an attorney," he said, looking at her with pity. "I am certain that you know the law, I hope."

The room became silent, the air thicker than the darkest fog over the mountains on a cold winter morning.

"Thank you," Celia said to the policeman.

Mother and daughter drove home quietly, feeling ashamed and terribly disturbed.

From that moment on, Celia made space for super quality time with Amanda. They walked on the beach. Once a week they ate vegetarian pizzas and salad at the tiny Italian restaurant a mile from their home. They went to the gym together as often as they could. That very night was a nightmare in the past, yet today so graciously appreciated.

BREAK TIME

FORMULA II

Parents: Tell your kids how special they are, regardless of what they have done or not done.

A Brief Reminder

It was August. Mark had just turned fifteen the week before. His birthday always felt special to him, but not this year. His skin had changed. It was not as clear and clean looking as in years past. He was going through some normal hormonal changes, and his face was proof of that. It was reddish and pimples appeared everywhere. Mark hated the way he looked; even more so, the way he felt. He was somewhat confused. Deep inside, he knew very well the reasons why his face changed so much, but he preferred to close himself off from the world and hide from reality. He locked himself in his room for hours after school and on weekends. He did not answer his friends' calls and declined to go to the movies with them. He felt depressed and had no desire to talk to anyone, trying to sort out his troubled mind independently.

His parents, Tina and Jeff, had lots of responsibilities to juggle. They were a typical young couple managing the family life to the best of their knowledge.

They had three younger children: a five-year-old girl and nine-year-old twins. Tina worked the evening shift as a waitress at a coffee shop while Jeff was home with the kids. He had a daytime job as a car mechanic for European auto-mobiles. The arrangement seemed practical and logical to them. They alternated their time with the kids at home. Sometimes they would both stay overtime to generate more cash for savings so they could purchase a larger home. Even though they were completely grateful to own one in the first place, realistically, the thirteen hundred square-foot homes with two bathrooms became too small for their family of six.

Tina and Jeff were hardworking parents and so busy most of the time that they did not notice the change in Mark's behavior or the change in his complexion. Routine life occupied their full attention, and Mark was getting more and more lost and lonely as the days passed by.

And so it happened that on one of those normal week-nights while Tina was serving the customers at the counter, an old lady with an unusually pleasant look took a seat at the end of the row. She had snow white hair pulled in a bun, a pale thin face, and dark brown eyes. She was wearing a thick, white cotton blouse and a long gray skirt with buttons all the way down. She seemed elegant and quite neat. Tina was touched by her presence and asked the woman what she could get for her. She was intrigued by her looks, and the lady responded with an unfamiliar accent, "A cup of hot tea and wheat toast with some cream cheese will be just fine for me."

Tina confirmed the request and, within minutes, served the lady her food and tea. The lady looked different from the usual customers she had served throughout the years. She had an aura of contentment on her soft face.

Tina suddenly had an urge to know more about this lady. She got up all her courage and asked politely, "Are you from this area? I've never seen you before."

"No," the lady responded, almost in a whisper, "I came to San Francisco to visit the Golden Gate Bridge. Funny you should ask. It took me many years to get here. An old dream fulfilled at the age of 70. I live far away from here. Other responsibilities much more meaningful and important took priority on my list, so here I am now, and I do feel a sense of accomplishment," she said with a big smile.

Tina probed deeper. "Do you have children?" she asked with great concern.

"Yes, I do indeed," the old lady answered quickly, "and I have the fortune to have grandchildren, too. Three of them as a matter of fact. They are teenagers, fourteen, sixteen, and seventeen, and they all live with me."

Tina became even more inquisitive. "How come? Where are the parents?"

"My son wants to live a free life, and their mother is even more free-spirited. They have no time or place for the kids, especially now. My son moved to South America, and their mother changes homes more often than I care to say. I wonder if she'll ever settle down."

"You see, my dear," the old lady continued, "they don't want to bother with the kids, but I ." With a broad smile and sparkling eyes she added, "They are very special to me, and I love them so."

"Thank you for those words. I needed to hear them," Tina responded, feeling a rush, wanting to give the lady a warm hug. She felt close to her.

When Tina drove home that night after her tiring shift, she felt eager and anxious to see the kids in the morning before they left for school. It was Mark's chore to give them breakfast during the week and drive them to their respective schools. That very morning, Tina woke up early and greeted them in the kitchen with a big smile on her face. She was preparing toast, eggs, bacon, and freshly squeezed orange juice for them, feeling energetic. The kids and Jeff were a bit surprised at her expression.

As they all sat down at the kitchen table, she looked at each child with softness in her eyes, and the world around them shined like the brightest diamonds in a dark, starless night.

"You are all so special to me," she said with teary eyes. "I love you all so much, today and always."

Her children knew that she meant every word she said. They did not question it. "We love you, too, Mom," they all answered quickly, and breakfast tasted better to them than ever before.

Mark registered the genuine words, and he carried them with him every single day from that moment on. He understood that he was loved, and he paid less and less attention to his face. Shortly after, his skin started to clear up, and the reflection in his bathroom mirror became more appealing and kind. His nights became less lonely, and he filled them with happy thoughts, erasing the worry and the emptiness, knowing that he was indeed special.

FORMULA III

Teenagers: Parents are not the enemy!

Repeat the following statement:

My parent's love and care about me from the very first moment. My presence brings them joy and happiness.

BELIEVE THAT!

You must repeat in your mind the following words:

My mom and dad care for me. They were teenagers once, too.

Listen to what your parents have to say. Parents care deeply. Friends may as well, but they will never have love. The parental role is one of a kind. You earn it for a lifetime.

It's a fact.

Please do not get irritated when they speak to you or ask you a question. Do not take this as an inquisition. Your parents want to connect with you, and now that you are nearing adulthood, they need to feel that they are still needed.

How wonderful it is to embrace the connection. The best years are now, when you are still home, maybe in your first year or second year of college. You are grown up, yet you do not have to carry the responsibilities of an adult. This is a transitional period between the chapters.

These years are incredibly rich. Keep them that way.

A short story:

Sam left for school in June. It was his choice to move to the East Coast from Huntington Beach, California. His parents rented a big truck, hauling his bedroom furniture, the TV/stereo, and all his books and personal belongings. They wanted to make this transition as smooth as possible.

When everything was settled in his new place, his mother placed an old photo on his small bookcase. The photo was taken on a trip to Mexico several years earlier, and they were all smiling and looking tanned and very relaxed. Sam knew that his parents were there for him every step of the way, and he was certain that they loved and cared for him. They would miss him, indeed, but all they wanted for him was true happiness, fulfillment of his dreams and goals without selfish motives, guilt, and demands.

FORMULA IV

Parents: Teach your children LOVE education and cover the topic of sex afterwards.

School studies cover sex education on the surface. They touch on some of the details of human anatomy and the modern methods of preventing pregnancy and disease. Though important, they lack the equally important education about love, what should be the driving force that brings two people together in physical union. It does not work the other way around. Teens learn about real love in their home, observing the different types of love that exists among family members, especially the romantic love between parents.

So, what about LOVE?

When is the proper time to discuss this topic? Indeed, a teenager needs to be enlightened on the subject to gain understanding. They are ready to receive.

As parents, we must have some knowledge of it. I hope we do.

So, let's talk about LOVE education. Is there love among teenagers? Or is there a competition for attention or a rush to get to a car or bedroom to engage in a fun game called "Sex"?

Sadly enough, teenagers are not properly educated in love. As soon as their bodies begin changing, they become interested in sex, desiring attention, acknowledgment, and love. Like a drug, once the idea and experience of sex enters their consciousness, they become numb to the effect and disregard the impact it has on their lives.

Then comes the moment they were sure would never happen to them—teenage pregnancy—bringing with it despair and decisions that need to be made in the midst of that dark storm. What are we going to do? And, indeed, the poor choices are made. Why? Teenagers do not know what to do, lacking the experience and maturity to make decisions on such matters, and the parents are often outside the loop of reality.

It is all because of the pure fact that teenagers today do not understand the concept of love. They care for one another, act as if they respect one another, but the maturity comes much later.

Therefore, teenagers today jump into sex without the knowledge of love, so where will this act lead them?

In today's social climate, it has become normal and acceptable to be sexually active at a young age.

KIDS are having sex with other kids, with both the opposite sex and the same sex. Experimenting with the newness and excitement of sex, yet completely unaware of love, true closeness, and how magical sex is meant be.

To address this very special topic, try the following:

Parents:

♦ Express and teach your teenagers what love is all about.

♦ Ask your teenagers what they know about love.

♦ Be an example. If you are married, act in a loving manner with your spouse. If you are a single parent, use discretion. Seek love through intimacy, with sex as the result of that love.

Teenagers:

♦ Ask your parents how they define love and when they became aware of the feeling?

♦ Try to understand the meaning of love and the adornment called sex.

♦ You are very vulnerable, and therefore, without the understanding of love, you cannot possibly make well-grounded decisions.

♦ Do not rush into sex.

Teenagers who take the step towards commitment often spread apart soon after. In very few cases does the relationship last.

Sex is the hot fire on the stove that should not be touched carelessly by kids.

LOVE IS A FEELING, and only a feeling.

True love is a large tree planted securely in the ground, bearing the sweetest fruits, and the branches are:

- Honesty

- Respect

- Loyalty

- Intimacy

Parents: How do you set an example in your own relationships, encouraging ones built on love rather than sex?

- Understand one another.

- Support one another.

- Compromise when the situation calls for it.

- Validate one another's feelings and views.

- Give attention to one another, even in the busiest of times.

- Talk to each other; share your inner thoughts and goals.

- Discuss your fears and concerns, without hesitation.

◆ Be there for one another, rain or shine.

◆ Help one another wherever you need support.

◆ Do not belittle your partner, and do not judge them in the heat of the moment; that is when mistakes are made.

◆ Do not get angry at one another—address the issue calmly.

◆ Spend quality time together.

◆ Share some hobbies together.

◆ Give space to one another—do not lose your identity.

◆ When one of you is sick, be there for them.

◆ When money is tight, do not put all your energy into how much you would like to have; built financial security as a team.

◆ Go on vacations together.

◆ Plan together and design your goals together.

- Respect extended family members.

- If you do not have something good to say, be silent.

- Compliments are great; be truthful and have integrity.

- Surprise each other with little gifts, without a special reason or occasion.

- Be warm with one another, affectionate, and never take each other for granted.

- Treat your partner every day like it is your first date.

And when you do eventually make love with your partner, touch them with all of your heart and soul, while you seal it with your physical body.

Now, let me ask you a question?

Is a teenager capable of absorbing, understanding, and following all of the above?

When parents prepare the solid foundation of love and sex, the teenager's actions will follow automatically toward that very same direction, and they will be much happier, less troubled, and less confused.

Then they will mature and become parents themselves. They will bring the same teachings into their reality, sharing the understanding with the new teenage generation.

Let me repeat it one more time.

AS WE ALREADY KNOW:

Love is a feeling followed by actions moving the circle in a slow motion.

Sex is a purely physical act on its own. Yes, it is multifaceted, but the end result is the same.

Sex is an act spinning around love, and when this act is a stand-alone physical performance, it is incomplete. Only with the feelings and the emotion of love will sex become real, fantastic, uplifting, taking you higher than anything else in this world.

Love is the seed growing forever; sex is the fruit tasting sweet.

We all know this so well, yet we forget to share our knowledge, experiences, and understanding with the most important people in our lives:

Our kids—the teenagers.

When love fails, leaves us, or perhaps never really existed, the physical need of sex, the weakness, becomes a lonely feeling after the act, and the emptiness can be unbearable at times.

We are born to feel, we are designed to give, we live beautifully when we love, and we continue our endless search for sex, like an addiction, breathing and sealing our longing before our time.

A second lesson on the education of love:

DO NOT teach your kids anger; there is too much out there up for grabs. Teach them beauty, values, faith, and positive attitudes instead.

Make certain that you discuss with them and participate with them in all major changes, such as changing jobs, moving to another city, purchasing a new home, or bringing another child into the family. If you are a single parent, you must introduce your kids to the significant other if you are considering marrying or setting up a full-time partnership.

These changes are affecting their lives, just as much as yours. When you let them participate, they will feel not only included and considered, but they will also acquire a sense of security and confidence beyond belief.

You must be gentle and soft spoken when you address a subject with your teenagers. You know the saying, "It's not what you say, but how you say it." Always examine your words and your tone before speaking. Your children are the most precious people in your life. Treat them that way. Catch yourself before the words come out sounding too harsh.

Remember at all times, it is not easy to be a teenager. There is so much they need to deal with. The modern world out there is a slippery path. Try to understand how they think, how sensitive they are. Where do they run? Why are they so addicted to technology, and how can we change that?

When you are too tired or troubled by major issues, you should not lose your cool with them. They can see that you are not at your best, and most of the time they feel help-less, with a deep need for you to guide them without asking for it. Read between the expressions in their eyes.

Business Travel

Fred came home from a three-week sales seminar in Asia. Sheila was anxious to have some private time with her husband. She had to juggle a lot while he was gone: the kids, the house, and her part-time nursing job at the hospital.

Without even realizing it, she was screaming at her 14-year-old daughter, Tiffany, "Go see your room! It's a mess! Don't come out till it's totally clean and all your clothes are picked up!"

Tiffany shouted back, "Stop yelling at me!"

"I know you're frustrated. I'm happy to see Dad back home, but at the same time I was so anxious about having him back here with us," Tiffany added. "I don't feel like a family when he is away."

The room became silent. The faces changed. Tiffany walked slowly towards her room and closed the door quietly. Sheila and Fred looked at each other. They stood still and, within minutes, knocked on Tiffany's door together.

She opened it.

"Sorry," Sheila said extending her arms to her daughter. "Do you need some help?" she asked. "It's quicker to put everything away with six arms," she added.

"Okay," Tiffany responded.

The evening turned to a calm peaceful mood, and the fried chicken with the mashed potatoes they shared for dinner tasted so wonderfully good. And, a deeper understanding kept them bonded more than ever before.

FORMULA V

Teenagers: Ask your parents questions and listen to their answers.

Who says that kids don't need answers to so many issues concerning them? Ask your parents questions about matters dear to your heart, such as school, social status, your looks, your feelings, or your work. Do not hesitate to do so. You are not a burden. Do not feel that you are bothering them. You have the right to know. Your parents should never feel bothered when you seek their support or their help. It is always a pleasure for parents to give guidance and know that, due to the past experiences, they just might have the proper answer for you. A simple worry can be erased in a second. How would you know how to solve a problem that never existed before? Experience is one of our greatest treasures.

Walk a step closer to them and reality will shine brighter as the days flow in and out.

FORMULA VI

Parents: Get involved in you children's world!

- Ask them what type of music they like. Purchase it and put it on in the car.

- When you go shopping, ask them to join you. See what type of clothes they like. Catch their style. Help them with it.

- Stop for a cold drink or a hot cup of chocolate in the midst of shopping…takes a break.

- Invite your children's friends for a meal or dessert.

- See who they hang around with.

- Get to know their friends' parents.

- Teach the kids the importance of choosing the "right friends" and what that means.

- Ask you kids if they need help with their homework.

- BE THEM FOR A DAY!

FORMULA VII

Parents: Never use these dark statements:

♦ I had it much harder than you.

♦ My life was much more boring than yours.

♦ I NEVER had the things you have today.

♦ You are costing us too much.

♦ You are too lazy.

♦ I can hardly wait until you leave the house.

♦ I should NEVER have had you.

♦ You will never be me.

♦ Can't you see how you look?

♦ Why can't you be smarter?

♦ You must get straight A's, or else.

- If you continue as you are now, you will never be a success.

- You are too spoiled.

- Wait until your father hears this.

- Stop talking on the phone so much.

- You are too disorganized.

- Where is your mind? You are always somewhere else.

- I will never buy you a car if you…

- Stop! What are you doing right now? Follow me.

- You don't care about anything.

- Other girls your age are much more developed.

- Sex is a subject we are not talking about in this house.

- I don't love you anymore.

- Parents always know better.

11-Step Formula to Bridge the Gap Between Parents and Teenagers

- Don't ask me for more money.

- You eat too much.

- Don't ask me for anything, I am too busy.

- I don't like who you've become.

- Who cares if you like my boy/girlfriend? (Single parents)

- NO more TV for you the entire week.

- I took your computer away. It's in storage for now.

- Here is thirty dollars. Go somewhere, just leave me alone.

- Stay out of my sight. I don't care where you go, just go.

- You are a terrible driver. I am taking the car keys away for good.

- Stop asking for more clothes. I don't care about fashion and the way your friends dress.

- Don't ask me for anything to borrow. What's mine is mine.

♦ Your father/mother used to do that. That is why we are no longer married. (Divorced parents)

♦ You can't go visit your father. He's a loser. (Divorced parents)

♦ Your mother is a tramp and very selfish. (Divorced parents)

♦ If you think you are so smart, then why do you do so many foolish things?

♦ You could never do my job.

Divorced parents: Do not use your kids as ping-pong balls!

Single parents: Do no complain about how hard it is for you!

All parents: Do not brag about your kids while you overwhelm them with activities. Do house chores or your home business chores as a team.

INTERMISSION

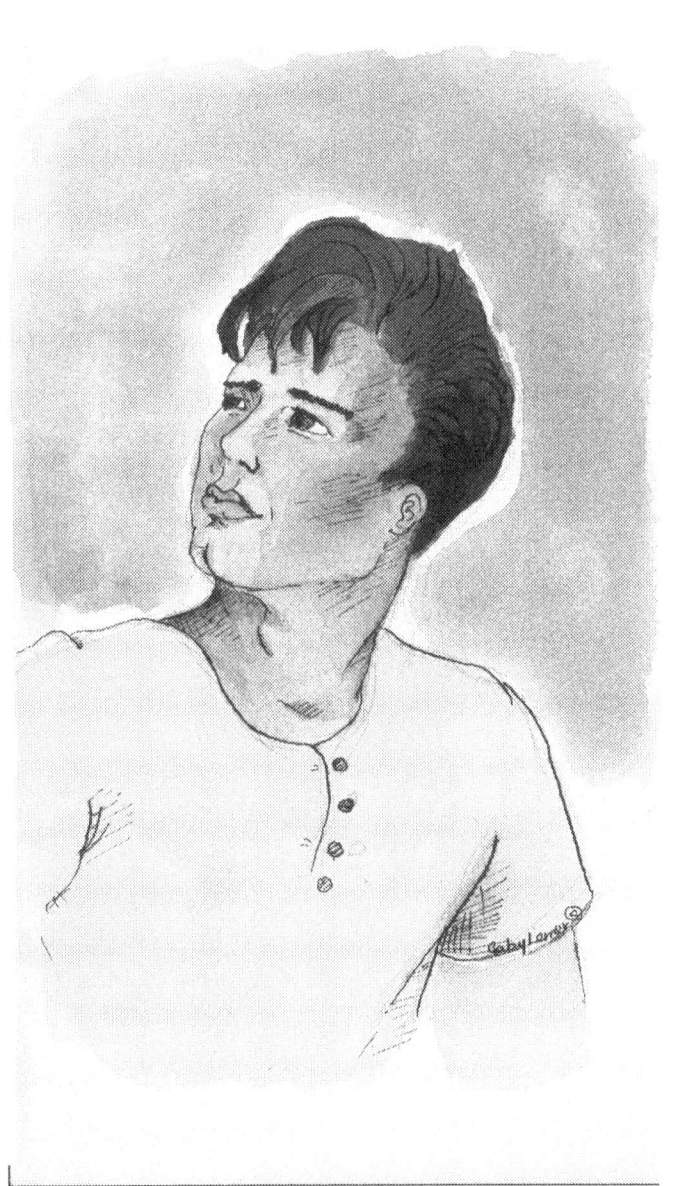

FORMULA VIII

Parents: Do not punish teenagers.

The key is to make them understand how consequences have a powerful impact on our day-to-day lives (the practical aspect of actions).

When you punish your teenage kids, you shut off your connection to them that can be achieved with a soft touch. You are aware of your actions whether you accept them or not. There is no reason to add to the weight of the problem by adding more negativity to it. On the contrary, when you soften a hard spot, you relieve the pressure, releasing it, and the problem will be allowed to pass rather than repeat itself. Concentrating on the unacceptable act with fear of or from punishment will result in it being repeating over and over again. Instead of learning to influence a situation using strength and good, the teenager will turn toward rebellion just to prove that fear does not help and love was not there in the first place. A vindictive response, however, it will only backfire and hurt the teen in the long run. Gentle teachings will always bring out the brighter picture. Educate your kids instead of punishing them, showing authority and reason. Receiving more knowledge will make them understand the outcome with a kind heart.

Judgment is a form of punishment as well. Do not judge. Present the facts as they are manifested, as well as the reality and the choices.

There is a time and place for discussion and clarification, without the weight of judgment and punishment. A parent or guardian must prepare the foundation to good, solid discipline years before the child enters the difficult teenage period. Discuss serious topics together and agree to them as a family unit—without fear.

As parents, we feel better by doing so, and the teenager will experience deeper insight that will last a lifetime.

FORMULA IX

Parents: Discuss with your teenager the topic of taking a part-time job.

There are several good reasons to follow this path:

♦ Learning the value of money.

♦ Understanding the differences between school and work.

♦ Experiencing communication among people in the workplace.

♦ Filling in the leftover time between school and social activities with proper direction.

♦ Building within them a sense of self-worth, confidence, and independence.

♦ Learning to respect their superiors, a special discipline that falls outside the parameters of family life.

♦ Enriching academic learning with hands-on experience.

- Determining whether their field of interest is truly the direction in life they would like to take.

- Reducing selfishness by learning to share space and a variety of commodities with others.

- Providing them with a sense of pride and contentment with their achievements.

Do not ask them for the money they have earned. Teach them to save a percentage of it. The balance should be for enjoyment and entertainment.

SUPPORT them throughout the course of life when a good cause is presented.

HELP them with funds for education when your finances allow.

The parent-child journey is the most magical aspect of it all. ENJOY and love every second of it. You will both feel joyful, youthful, healthy, and strong when the passage is fruitful and colorful. After all, our society is too wrapped up in the destination. By forgetting to breathe in and catch the shifting seasons of life, we fail to realize that it is the journey, not the destination, that matters.

We can conquer the unexpected and uncontrollable events when we feel complete; knowing that the bond is there allows us to be tolerant of the darker times, the shades that we pass as we climb the ladder of life higher and higher. Knowing we are not alone gives us the strength to continue regardless of what life presents us.

We reach the top more swiftly when each step we take is a steady one, and smiles from within greet the new day, keeping us the present at all times.

Plan for tomorrow wisely. Short-term goals and long-term goals are indeed a smart approach, but be careful not to get completely swept away into the future. One must live TODAY…and when tomorrow comes, that TODAY will repeat itself naturally.

FORMULA X

Parents: Give your teenage kids CHOICES.

Please do not impose on them the following:

- The profession you think they should choose.

- The college or university you think they should go to.

- Where they should live.

- Who they should date.

- Whether they should marry young or wait until they are older.

- Which car they should drive.

- How often they should call you.

- How much they should weigh and whether they are too thin or too fat.

- What they should eat.

- What hairstyle they should wear.

- What type of music they should listen to.

- How they should spend their money.

Present them with choices, using common sense. You may color them and add weight to them, but present the choices accurately along with their potential consequences.

Do not live your dreams through their lives. You made your choices.

Let them pick a profession for which they have passion.

Let them enjoy their youth.

Let them talk to you and explain to you who they are. They are NOT you!

Let them express and release their frustrations and their views on matters close to their hearts.

Show them the various choices out there and the potential outcomes with reason. When the options are presented in a calm, realistic fashion, teenagers are exposed to them in a proper light and will make the right decision that fits their own mold.

Occasionally they will change paths, and that is okay, too.

Sometimes we feel that one skill is pulling us closer than another. Only when we experience using the skill firsthand will we be able to realize whether or not it is what we had in mind in the first place.

When we choose to work in a profession closer to our hearts, we will be more likely to excel, and our results will be of higher quality. The money will follow, without concern over whether or not that is of most importance to us.

Teenagers: Please do not be followers.

Each and every one of you is a living piece of a grand puzzle. We search for different things when there is no room for jealousy or competition.

We are all gifted and special in various fields of knowledge. You must follow your own desire and path as an exclusive design selected for you only. You may be influenced or hear a good idea that is appealing to you, yet you may develop the idea and ultimately create an entirely different shape and effect. We do learn from others exposing opinions. Different perceptions and arguments are healthy.

BE YOURSELF. It fits you. It is your size. Celebrate the special time in your life.

With good, healthy, loving communication with parents, you will know who you are and where you want to reach, understanding the challenges you will have to conquer along the way.

ENHANCE IT WITH MUSIC…The melody will warm your soul. I promise you that.

FORMULA XI

Teenagers and Parents: Plan a getaway together.

Big or small, vacations are the perfect time to relax and connect:

♦ School pressure is gone.

♦ Work is out of sight.

♦ Household chores are left at home.

♦ A change of view is an incredible venture on its own—another image of YOU in the mirror.

♦ A vacation refreshes and rejuvenates the mind and body.

You will discover new feelings, thoughts, impressions, hobbies, foods, cultures, expressions, unfamiliar sites, photographs to cherish in your mind, languages, roads, maps, vegetation, trees, fruits, music, diets, other methods of exercising, dancing, and treasures of a special kind… TOGETHER.

A WHOLE NEW WORLD opened just for you. And you will come home a NEW YOU.

It's quite cool to go on vacation with your parents…

You will find out that you actually know each other and respect each other, and that you are confident and tall, keeping your head up high.

Love the moments, looking forward to the next one with so much more exuberance, knowing that you passed the challenge with flying colors, both sides of the bridge holding a flag of the same material.

WE BELONG!

How lucky for us that we do. The only difference is that for parents, the journey ahead is a bit shorter, the past is full of knowledge, and yet we still have so much to learn and absorb. Ride the waves of life with our children together.

Teenagers: Your journey is beginning with so much to look forward to, living today with incredible understanding and a sense of belonging even though you are so capable of independence.

Is there anything more meaningful or fulfilling than the feeling that we belong? We are connected, and the ribbon that connects us will follow as a natural course.

Show each other that there is true love, and with true actions of love and love education, we will not fall.

But even if we stumble on a sharp stone while walking on the clean white sand, we will learn and experience how to walk forward.

To love is to be grateful for today, for the NOW, and for all the tomorrows.

And that special fountain of love between parents and children, can you ever describe it completely with words?

The answer is simple and kind:

We love each other as much as we possibly can!

It is easy when we grow from the same seed anyway.

A poem for you:

As I opened my door to you
Butterflies were flying around us in groups of two
Regally dressed with gold and amber
Among the violets swaying the musical path
As we hugged the entrance of a new day
Without a speckle of doubt in our clear minds

You followed me without questions.

THERE was love
And the answers were filling the missing dots
A journey never forgotten
While the dark nights couldn't escape our enduring love

To my children and their children

Love will bond us for always
We taste it along the way

With honey on our lips
We will seal the marked envelope
Without a stamp
Reaching the destination anyway…
So why not?
Love for now and then…

Voices without a sound
And an echo filled with hope
Somehow even in the dark.

11-STEP FORMULA RECAP

1. **Teenagers and Parents:** Spend one to two hours a week of quality time outside your home. Pick the place together. Make time for it.

2. **Parents:** Tell your teenagers how special they are as often as you can.

3. **Teenagers:** Parents are not the enemy. Express your gratitude and love for them.

4. **Parents:** Teach your teenaged kids LOVE EDUCATION and cover the topic of sex afterwards.

5. **Teenagers:** Ask your parents' questions and listen.

6. **Parents:** Get involved in your kid's world today.

7. **Parents:** Do not direct dark statements at your kids. It will destroy their self-esteem and confidence. They need to get ready to go out into the real world.

8. **Parents:** Do not punish your teenagers. Analyze before judging.

9. **Parents:** Guide your kids to desire part-time work during their school years for a healthy perspective.

10. **Parents:** Present your kids with choices in life.

11. **Teenagers and Parents:** Plan vacation time once a year. Get away together. It's a cool thing to do.

A NOTE TO THE READER

I trust that during the time of reading this book, *11-Step Formula to Bridge the Gap between Parents and Teenagers*, lots of stimulating questions opened up in your mind as well as answers to so many areas of doubts you build during your course as a parent or a teenager.

My main goal is to reach out to all parents and teenagers clearly and expose the relationship with more sensitivity and understanding, while facing reality with more lightness and love. This topic has been a battling unfinished issue for decades. We need to address it with great importance so the bridging can be accomplished.

If I only touched twenty to twenty-five percent of you out there, I feel that we are on the right track. The rest will follow. We, in general, prefer to live happier lives. Why wouldn't we choose that path?

I enjoyed sharing with you my own experience and the collective profound outcome of hundreds of parents and teenagers interviewed around the world.

It has been delightfully fun, and the results of this study can be fruitful for you, too.

Be open-minded and be updated with the most current lifestyle of teenagers today.

Thank you.

Ana H.B. Weber

ABOUT THE AUTHOR

Ana Hermina Weber was born in Romania and has been living in the United States since 1974. Among other passions, she loves to write, expressing a purpose of love and beauty to her readers. Her main goal is to reach out to parents with teenagers, bridging the gap between them; quite a noble cause.

She has also written *Dumped: The Ultimate Guide to Starting Over*, a wonderful, uplifting approach with a fantastic, healthy attitude, creating the best results for all ages and types of individuals experiencing this dramatic change at least once in their lives.

She has also released *Avantgarde*, a novel based on a true story, and a contemporary book of poems entitled *Silky Emotions, LEMONS into Lemonade without the Sugar*.

The above photo was taken in Florence, Italy, at the Pontevecchio Bridge, a magical place to visit, recommended to all parents and teenagers.

978-0-595-40717-0
0-595-40717-X